Discrete Mathematics Simplified

Discrete Mathematics Simplified

Cornelio Jeremy G. Ecle

Arvin Anthony S. Araneta

Alma Padit Kuizon

Cherlowen A. Bolito

1st Special Edition
Innovative Research Initiative and Beyond

June 2021
Systenext Alpha Research and Innovations Limited © 2021

Discrete Mathematics Simplified
Fundamental Principles of Discrete Mathematics
By Cornelio Jeremy G. Ecle, Arvin Anthony S. Araneta, Alma Padit Kuizon
and Cherlowen A. Bolito

"Topic notice: The topics presented in this book were generated using ChatGPT, an artificial intelligence language model. ChatGPT has been trained on a vast amount of data and can generate informative and engaging topics for a variety of subjects. While the topics have been carefully selected and reviewed, they may not be entirely accurate or complete. The purpose of this book is to explore the capabilities of language models and their potential to generate informative content."

Warning and Disclaimer

"Warning: This book includes content that was generated by an artificial intelligence language model, ChatGPT. While ChatGPT has been trained on a vast amount of data and can provide valuable insights and information, the content may not be entirely accurate or complete. The information in this book should be used for educational or entertainment purposes only and should not be relied upon as a substitute for professional advice.

Disclaimer: The author and publisher of this book make no representations or warranties with respect to the accuracy, completeness, or reliability of the information contained herein. The information is provided "as is" without warranty of any kind, and the author and publisher shall not be liable for any damages whatsoever arising out of the use of or inability to use this information, even if they have been advised of the possibility of such damages."The authors cannot be held responsible to any person or entity, for any damage or loss arising from the information and in reference to the technical details mentioned on this book.

ISBN: 9798434958097

Acknowledgement

"I would like to acknowledge the contribution of ChatGPT, an artificial intelligence language model, to the research and inspiration for this book. ChatGPT provided valuable information and insights that helped shape my understanding of the topics covered in this book. I am grateful for the support of the team behind ChatGPT, who have created a powerful tool that has enriched my writing experience."

Dedication

The author wishes to give thanks to the Creator for making this research work possible. An enormous and significant time has been dedicated in the full completion of this research work and the efforts for this research initiative continuous through time thus, the author acknowledges the gift of time and opportunity given by the great and almighty Creator.

Table of Contents

To the Creator.

AUTHOR'S NOTE

"Discreet Mathematics Simplified" provides a thorough introduction to the fundamental concepts and techniques of discrete mathematics. The book covers a broad range of topics, including logic, set theory, combinatorics, graph theory, and algorithms. It also includes numerous examples, exercises, and applications to computer science, cryptography, and other areas. Written in a clear and concise style, this book is ideal for undergraduate students in mathematics, computer science, and engineering who seek a solid foundation in discrete mathematics. With its comprehensive coverage and accessible approach, this book is an essential resource for anyone interested in the study of discrete mathematics."

CHAPTER ONE

Introduction to Discreet Mathematics

Discrete Mathematics is a branch of mathematics which deals with discrete objects, such as integers and finite sets. It focuses on mathematical structures that are fundamentally distinct from one another (as opposed to continuous quantities). Discrete math can be used in various fields including computer science, economics, engineering, and operations research. Some topics covered include logic, proof techniques, graph theory, combinatorics, probability, and algorithms.

A sample discreet math problem could involve finding the number of different ways 8 people can sit around a circular table if there must always be an odd number of people sitting at each seat. The answer would depend on whether or not the chairs are arranged in a clockwise direction or counter-clockwise direction. If the seats are arranged clockwise then there are 240 possible arrangements; however, if they are arranged counter-clockwise then there are only 165 possible arrangements since some configurations will have two people facing each other.

Elements of discrete mathematics include logic and proof techniques, set theory, graph theory, combinatorics, probability, algorithms and complexity analysis, cryptography, game theory, and computer science topics such as finite automata and Turing machines. Discrete mathematics also involves counting and enumeration, mathematical induction, recurrence relations, and Boolean algebra. Additionally, it includes applications to various fields including engineering, economics, operations research, artificial intelligence, and more.

Mathematical Induction is a method used in proofs which states that if a statement holds true for all values less than or equal to n (the current value), then it must be true for the current value itself. This can be applied to any type of function where the same result will always follow from repeated application of the same operation on smaller numbers. For example, proving that $2n + 1$ is an even number by showing that when $n = 0, 1, 2...$ it works out that $2(0) + 1 = 1, 2(1) + 1 = 3, 2(2) - 1 = 5$ etc., so therefore $2n+1$ must be an even number. Mathematical induction can be extended further with additional assumptions but this basic form is often enough to prove most statements.

Examples of mathematical induction include:

1. Proving that 2n + 1 is an even number as described above;

2. Showing that every positive integer is either divisible by another positive integer or is a multiple of all its digits;

3. Demonstrating that the sum of the first n terms of a geometric sequence is $(n/2)^n$;

4. Establishing that the product of two consecutive integers is divisible by four; and

5. Verifying that the sum of the squares of the first n natural numbers is $(n^2)/2$.

To prove this, we can use mathematical induction on the statement "2n+1 is an even number". We will assume it holds for some base case n = k, i.e., 2k+1 is an even number. Then, we need to show that if this is true then so must be the case for any larger value of n, i.e., 2(k+1)+1 is also an even number. This follows from the fact that 2k+1 multiplied by 2 gives us 2(k+1) which is an even number since 2k+1 was assumed to be one. Thus, our assumption holds for all values of n and thus the statement is proven.

This proof requires two lemmas. The first lemma states that given any non-zero natural number N, there exists at least one other natural number M such that N mod M equals zero (i.e., N %M=0). To prove this, let p and q be distinct primes with p >

q. Let A = {p^k *q^(N-k): k = 0...[log_p(N)]} and B = {p^l*q^(N-l): l = 0...[log_q(N)]}. Since p>q, [log_p(N)] < [log_q(N)] and similarly [log_q(N)]<[log_p(N)]. Therefore, A and B are disjoint sets and their union contains all numbers between 1 and N inclusive. By the pigeonhole principle, there exist two elements m and n in the set such that N mod m = 0 and N mod n = 0. These two elements satisfy the desired property.

The second lemma states that given any positive integer n, there exists a subset S of {1,...,9} such that n is equal to the sum of

The sum of the first n terms of a geometric sequence can be shown by using the formula for the sum of a geometric series, which states that Sn = 1/(1-r) * Sum[t^n]. In this case, r=1 and so S1 = 0 and Sn = 1/(1-1) * t^(n). Taking the power to the nth degree yields (n/2)^n as desired. Thus, demonstrating that the sum of the first n terms of a geometric sequence is (n/2)^n.

This statement can be established through mathematical proof or induction. Through mathematical proof, one could show that if x and y are consecutive integers then x + y = (x+y)/4. This follows from the fact that when adding two consecutive numbers together their difference must equal zero, meaning that they must have been evenly spaced on the number line. By dividing these two consecutive integers by four we get the result that the product of any two consecutive integers is divisible by four. Alternatively, induction can also establish this theorem since it requires proving that given some arbitrary integer n, the statement holds true for all positive integers greater than or equal to n. Therefore, either method will suffice in establishing that the product of two consecutive integers is divisible by four.

To verify this equation, one needs only to calculate the sum of the squares of the first n natural numbers. The formula for calculating this value is S=1/2*n*(n+1)*(2n+1). Plugging in values for n starting with 0 yields the following results:

S=(1/2)(0)+(1/2)(1)^2+(1/2)(2)=1

S=(1/2)(0)+(1/2)(1)^2+(1/2)(3)=9

S=(1/2)(0)+(1/2)(1)^2+(1/2)(4)=25

From this pattern, it is clear that the sum of the squares of the first n natural numbers is indeed (n^2)/2 as desired. Thus, verification has been successful.

Review Questions

1. What is discrete mathematics, and how is it different from continuous mathematics?

2. What are the basic principles of propositional logic, and how are they used in discrete mathematics?

3. What is set theory, and how is it used to study discrete structures?

4. How do we count and analyze combinations and permutations using combinatorics?

5. What is graph theory, and how is it used to model and analyze relationships between discrete objects?

6. What is the principle of mathematical induction, and how is it used to prove statements about discrete structures?

7. How are finite state machines and automata used to model and analyze discrete processes?

8. What is the significance of algorithms in discrete mathematics, and how are they used to solve problems?

9. How are discrete structures used in cryptography and computer science?

10. What are some real-world applications of discrete mathematics, such as in scheduling, network optimization, and game theory?

CHAPTER TWO

Topics in Discreet Mathematics

Discrete Mathematics Topics for Discussion in a University

1. Graph Theory and its applications
2. Combinatorics and Permutations
3. Algorithms and Complexity Analysis
4. Number Theory and Cryptography
5. Discrete Probability Distributions
6. Boolean Algebras and Logic Circuits
7. Matroid Theory
8. Game Theory
9. Optimization Techniques
10. Computational Geometry
11. Algorithm Design and Analysis
12. Machine Learning and Data Mining
13. Network Flow Models
14. Related Areas Of Computer Science And Engineering

The next discussion will be samples of the above mentioned topics in discreet mathematics,

1. Graph Theory and its applications

Graph theory is a branch of mathematics used to study networks, or graphs, consisting of nodes (vertices) connected by edges (links). It can be applied to many areas such as computer science, engineering, economics, sociology, etc., where one needs to analyze relationships between entities. Some common graph-theoretic concepts include paths, cycles, trees, connectivity, and network flow models. Applications of graph theory range from social media analysis to circuit design optimization.

Examples of Graph Theory is as follows.

1.1 Social Network Analysis - This involves analyzing connections between people in order to identify influential actors, detect clusters or communities within a network, and predict how information spreads through it.

1.2 Circuit Design Optimization – This uses graph theory to determine the shortest path for electrons to travel around a circuit while minimizing power consumption.

2. Combinatorics and Permutations

Permutation is an arrangement of objects into distinct patterns which are ordered according to some set of rules. Combinatorics deals with counting the number of possible arrangements or combinations of elements. For example, there are six permutations of the letters AABBCCDDEEFFG. The first letter could be A, B, C, D, E, F, G; each subsequent letter must follow the previous one in sequence. Therefore, there are six different permutations.

Examples of Combinatorics and Permutations is as follows.

Sample 1: Combinatorics

Question: A pizza place offers 10 toppings, but a customer can only choose 5 toppings for their pizza. How many different pizzas can be made?

Solution: To solve this problem, we need to use the formula for combinations, which is:

nCk = n! / (k! * (n - k)!)

where n is the total number of items, and k is the number of items we want to choose.

In this case, we have n = 10 (the number of toppings), and k = 5 (the number of toppings we want to choose). So, we can plug in these values and simplify:

10C5 = 10! / (5! * (10 - 5)!)

= 10! / (5! * 5!)

= (10 * 9 * 8 * 7 * 6) / (5 * 4 * 3 * 2 * 1)

= 252

Therefore, there are 252 different pizzas that can be made with 10 toppings if the customer can only choose 5 toppings.

Sample 2: Permutations

Question: In how many ways can the letters in the word "APPLE" be arranged?

Solution: To solve this problem, we need to use the formula for permutations, which is:

n! / (n - k)!

where n is the total number of items, and k is the number of items we want to arrange.

In this case, we have n = 5 (the number of letters in the word "APPLE"). We want to arrange all 5 letters, so k = 5. So, we can plug in these values and simplify:

5! / (5 - 5)!

= 5! / 0!

= 5!

Therefore, there are 5! = 120 ways to arrange the letters in the word "APPLE".

Review Questions

For Graph Theory

1. The Four Color Theorem: This theorem states that any map can be colored using only four colors such that no two adjacent regions have the same color. It is one of the most famous problems in graph theory, and was solved using computer-assisted proofs.

2. The Hamiltonian Path Problem: This problem asks whether a given graph contains a Hamiltonian path, which is a path that visits each vertex exactly once. It is a well-known NP-complete problem, and efficient algorithms are not known for large graphs.

3. The Traveling Salesman Problem: This problem asks for the shortest possible route that visits a given set of cities and returns to the starting point. It is also an NP-complete problem, and efficient algorithms are only known for small or special cases.

4. The Erdős–Faber–Lovász Conjecture: This conjecture states that any graph can be decomposed into a small number of "rainbow cycles", which are cycles that visit each vertex exactly once and have edges colored with distinct colors. It is related to the study of graph decompositions and combinatorial designs.

5. The P versus NP problem: This is one of the most famous open problems in computer science and mathematics. It asks whether there exists an efficient algorithm to solve all problems in the complexity class NP (problems that can be verified in polynomial time), or whether NP problems are fundamentally harder than problems in the class P (problems that can be solved in polynomial time). The problem has many implications for graph theory and other areas of combinatorics.

For Permutation and Combinatorics

1. The Riemann Hypothesis: This problem relates to the distribution of prime numbers and has connections to combinatorics through the study of the distribution of zeros of the Riemann zeta function.

2. The Hadamard Conjecture: This conjecture states that every matrix with entries +1 or -1 has determinant either +1 or -1. It is related to the study of permutations and their properties.

3. The Partition Problem: This problem asks how many ways a given number can be expressed as a sum of positive integers. It has connections to both combinatorics and number theory.

4. The Catalan Conjecture: This conjecture states that 8 and 9 are the only consecutive perfect powers, where a

perfect power is a number that can be written as an integer raised to a positive integer power. It is related to the study of permutations and their properties.

5. The Burnside Problem: This problem asks for the number of distinct colorings of a given object under a given group of symmetries. It has connections to both combinatorics and group theory.

6. The Nim Game: This is a two-player game where players take turns removing objects from piles, and the player who takes the last object wins. The game has connections to combinatorial game theory.

7. The Tutte Polynomial: This is a polynomial that is defined for graphs and encodes many interesting properties of the graph, including its chromatic polynomial, flow polynomial, and reliability polynomial. It has connections to both combinatorics and graph theory.

8. The de Bruijn Sequence: This is a sequence that contains every possible arrangement of a given set of symbols as a substring. It has connections to both combinatorics and coding theory.

9. The Schröder Number Problem: This problem asks how many ways a given number of objects can be arranged in noncrossing partitions. It has connections to both combinatorics and algebraic geometry.

10. The Stanley–Wilf Conjecture: This conjecture states that the number of permutations of a given length that avoid a certain pattern is bounded by a polynomial in the length of the permutation. It is related to the study of permutation patterns and their properties.

CHAPTER THREE

Topics in Discreet Mathematics

3. Algorithms and Complexity Analysis

Algorithm:

An algorithm is a set of instructions that can be followed to solve a specific problem or perform a particular task. It is a step-by-step approach to problem-solving, where each step is clearly defined and can be executed using a finite set of rules. Algorithms are widely used in computer science, mathematics, and engineering to solve complex problems efficiently.

An algorithm can be represented using various notations, such as pseudocode, flowcharts, and programming languages. The efficiency of an algorithm is measured by its time and space complexity, which is the amount of time and memory required to execute the algorithm.

Complexity Analysis:

Complexity analysis is the process of analyzing the performance of an algorithm in terms of its time and space complexity. It involves calculating the amount of time and memory required by an algorithm to solve a problem, as a function of the size of the input data.

Time complexity refers to the amount of time an algorithm takes to solve a problem, as a function of the size of the input data. It is usually measured using the Big O notation, which provides an upper bound on the worst-case running time of an algorithm.

Space complexity, on the other hand, refers to the amount of memory required by an algorithm to solve a problem, as a function of the size of the input data. It is also measured using the Big O notation, which provides an upper bound on the worst-case space usage of an algorithm.

By analyzing the time and space complexity of an algorithm, we can determine how efficient it is and compare it to other algorithms for the same problem. This allows us to choose the most appropriate algorithm for a given problem, based on its complexity and performance characteristics.

Sample:

Suppose you have an array of n integers, and you want to find the maximum element in the array. You can solve this problem using the following algorithm:

Algorithm:

1. Set max = A[0]
2. For i = 1 to n-1
   a. If A[i] > max
   i. Set max = A[i]
3. Return max

This algorithm works by initializing the maximum element to the first element of the array, and then iterating through the remaining elements of the array. If an element is found that is greater than the current maximum, then that element becomes the new maximum.

To analyze the time complexity of this algorithm, we can count the number of basic operations performed. The initialization step in line 1 takes one operation. The loop in lines 2-3 is executed n-1 times, and each iteration requires two operations (one comparison and one assignment). Therefore, the total number of operations is:

$$1 + 2(n-1) = 2n-1$$

Thus, the time complexity of this algorithm is O(n), which means that the worst-case running time of the algorithm grows linearly with the size of the input array.

To analyze the space complexity of this algorithm, we need to consider the amount of memory required to store the input array and the variables used by the algorithm. The input array requires n units of memory, and the variable max requires one unit of memory. Therefore, the space complexity of this algorithm is O(1), which means that the amount of memory required by the algorithm is constant and does not depend on the size of the input array.

4. Number Theory and Cryptography

Number Theory:

Number theory is a branch of mathematics that deals with the properties and relationships of numbers, particularly integers. It explores the patterns and structures that exist in numbers, as well as the ways in which they can be manipulated and combined.

Some of the key concepts in number theory include prime numbers, divisibility, congruences, and Diophantine equations. Number theory has many applications in computer science, cryptography, and other fields.

Cryptography:

Cryptography is the science of secure communication. It involves the use of mathematical algorithms to encrypt and decrypt messages, making them unintelligible to anyone who does not have the key to decipher them. Cryptography is used to ensure the confidentiality, integrity, and authenticity of messages sent over insecure channels, such as the internet.

There are two main types of cryptography: symmetric-key cryptography and public-key cryptography. In symmetric-key cryptography, the same key is used to encrypt and decrypt messages. In public-key cryptography, two different keys are used: a public key for encryption and a private key for decryption.

Cryptography has many practical applications, such as secure online transactions, secure communication between devices, and secure storage of sensitive information. It is an essential component of modern computer security.

Sample of Number Theory:

One of the fundamental concepts in number theory is prime numbers. A prime number is a positive integer greater than 1 that has no positive integer divisors other than 1 and itself. For example, 2, 3, 5, 7, and 11 are prime numbers.

One interesting problem in number theory is the question of how many prime numbers there are. It is known that there are infinitely many prime numbers, but it is not known exactly how many there are or how they are distributed among the integers.

Sample of Cryptography:

An example of a widely used cryptography algorithm is the Advanced Encryption Standard (AES). AES is a symmetric-key encryption algorithm that uses a block cipher to encrypt and decrypt messages. It was developed by the National Institute of Standards and Technology (NIST) and is used in many applications, including secure communications and data storage.

The AES algorithm works by dividing the message into blocks of 128 bits, and then applying a series of mathematical transformations to each block. These transformations are based on a secret key that is known only to the sender and receiver of the message. The resulting ciphertext is then transmitted over the network, and the receiver can use the same key to decrypt the message and recover the original plaintext.

AES is considered a very secure encryption algorithm, and it has been widely adopted by the industry and government agencies around the world. However, as with any cryptographic algorithm, its security is not absolute, and it is subject to attacks by skilled adversaries. Therefore, it is important to use proper key management and other security measures to ensure the integrity and confidentiality of encrypted messages.

Review Questions

For Algorithm

1. Longest Common Subsequence: Given two strings, find the length of the longest subsequence that is common to both strings. This is a classic problem in dynamic programming.

2. Dijkstra's Algorithm: Given a weighted graph with a starting node and an ending node, find the shortest path between the two nodes. Dijkstra's algorithm is a classic algorithm for solving this problem.

3. Merge Sort: Given an unsorted list of elements, sort the list in ascending order using the merge sort algorithm. This is a classic problem in sorting algorithms.

4. Minimum Spanning Tree: Given a weighted graph, find the tree that spans all nodes with the minimum total weight. This is a classic problem in graph algorithms, and there are many algorithms that can solve it, including Prim's algorithm and Kruskal's algorithm.

5. Knapsack Problem: Given a set of items with weights and values, and a knapsack of limited capacity, find the subset of items that maximizes the total value while keeping the total weight below the capacity of the knapsack. This is a classic problem in dynamic programming and optimization.

For Number Theory

1. Fermat's Last Theorem: This is a famous problem that states that there are no three positive integers a, b, and c that satisfy the equation $a^n + b^n = c^n$ for any integer value of n greater than 2.

2. Goldbach's Conjecture: This conjecture states that every even integer greater than 2 can be expressed as the sum of two prime numbers.

3. Collatz Conjecture: This is a conjecture that states that starting from any positive integer, the sequence obtained by repeatedly applying the function $n \rightarrow n/2$ if n is even or $n \rightarrow 3n + 1$ if n is odd, eventually reaches the number 1.

4. Quadratic Residues: Given an integer a and a prime number p, determine whether a is a quadratic residue modulo p, i.e., whether there exists an integer x such that $x^2 \equiv a \pmod{p}$.

5. Euler's Totient Function: Given a positive integer n, determine the number of positive integers less than or equal to n that are relatively prime to n. This is a fundamental function in number theory with many important applications.

CHAPTER FOUR

Topics in Discreet Mathematics

5. Discrete Probability Distributions

   Discrete probability distributions are a type of probability distribution that describes the probabilities of each possible outcome in a discrete set of values. A discrete set of values is one in which the values are distinct and separate, with no intermediate values possible.

   In a discrete probability distribution, each possible outcome is assigned a probability that represents the likelihood of that outcome occurring. The sum of all the probabilities in the distribution must be equal to 1.

   Examples of discrete probability distributions include the binomial distribution, the Poisson distribution, and the geometric distribution. These distributions are used to model a wide range of phenomena, such as the number of successes in a series of independent trials, the number of events occurring in a fixed time interval, and the number of trials required to achieve a single success.

Discrete probability distributions are important in many fields, including statistics, finance, and engineering. They are used to make predictions, estimate probabilities, and model real-world phenomena, and they provide a powerful tool for analyzing and understanding the behavior of random variables.

Sample 1: The Binomial Distribution

The binomial distribution is a discrete probability distribution that describes the number of successes in a fixed number of independent trials. It is often used to model phenomena such as the number of defective products in a sample, or the number of individuals in a population with a certain characteristic.

For example, let's say a manufacturing company produces 1,000 light bulbs, and each bulb has a 95% chance of being defect-free. We can model the probability distribution of the number of defect-free bulbs using the binomial distribution. If we define a "success" as a defect-free bulb, then the probability of success in each trial is 0.95, and the probability of failure is 0.05. If we randomly select 100 bulbs for testing, the binomial distribution can tell us the probabilities of getting 90, 91, 92, and so on, up to 100 defect-free bulbs.

Sample 2: The Poisson Distribution

The Poisson distribution is a discrete probability distribution that describes the number of events occurring in a fixed time interval. It is often used to model phenomena such as the number of phone calls received by a call center in an hour, or the number of cars passing through a toll booth in a minute.

For example, let's say a call center receives an average of 10 calls per hour. We can model the probability distribution of the number of calls using the Poisson distribution. The Poisson distribution tells us the probabilities of getting 0, 1, 2, and so on, up to some maximum number of calls, in a given hour. This information can help the call center to plan staffing levels and allocate resources effectively.

6.   Boolean Algebras and Logic Circuits

Boolean algebra is a branch of algebra that deals with binary variables, i.e., variables that can take on only one of two values, typically represented as 0 and 1. Boolean algebra provides a set of rules and operations for manipulating binary variables and expressions, including AND, OR, and NOT operations.

Boolean logic circuits are electronic circuits that use Boolean algebra to perform logical operations. They are used in a wide range of electronic devices, including computers, calculators, and digital signal processors.

A logic circuit is a circuit that performs a specific logical operation, such as AND, OR, or NOT. These circuits can be combined to create more complex circuits that perform more sophisticated operations. The basic building blocks of a logic circuit are logic gates, which are electronic components that perform a logical operation on one or more binary inputs to produce a binary output.

Examples of logic gates include AND gates, OR gates, and NOT gates. An AND gate produces a binary output of 1 only if both of its inputs are 1. An OR gate produces a binary output of 1 if either or both of its inputs are 1. A NOT gate produces the opposite of its input.

By combining these logic gates in various ways, more complex logic circuits can be built, such as adders, multiplexers, and flip-flops. These circuits are the building blocks of modern digital electronics and are essential to the operation of computers, smartphones, and other digital devices.

Sample: Designing a Logic Circuit for a Simple Alarm System

Let's say we want to design a simple alarm system that sounds an alarm if a door or window is opened. We can use Boolean algebra and logic circuits to design a circuit that detects when a door or window is opened and sounds an alarm.

First, we define our binary variables:

A = Door status (0 = closed, 1 = open)
B = Window status (0 = closed, 1 = open)
C = Alarm status (0 = off, 1 = on)
Next, we define the logical operations that will be used:

OR: This operation will be used to detect if the door or window is open.

NOT: This operation will be used to turn on the alarm when the door or window is open.

Using these operations, we can define the following Boolean expressions:

Door or window is open: A OR B

Alarm should be on when door or window is open: NOT(A OR B) = (NOT A) AND (NOT B)

Using these expressions, we can design a logic circuit as follows:

Connect the inputs A and B to an OR gate.

Connect the output of the OR gate to the inputs of a NOT gate.

Connect the output of the NOT gate to the input of an AND gate.

Connect the output of the AND gate to the input of a speaker or other alarm device.

When the door or window is open, the OR gate produces a binary output of 1. This output is then inverted by the NOT gate to produce a binary output of 0. This output is then fed into the AND gate along with the binary output of 0 from the other input (since the alarm is initially off). The AND gate produces a binary output of 0, which turns off the speaker or other alarm device.

When the door or window is closed, the OR gate produces a binary output of 0. This output is inverted by the NOT gate to produce a binary output of 1. This output is then fed into the AND gate along with the binary output of 0 from the other input (since the alarm is initially off). The AND gate produces a binary output of 0, which keeps the speaker or other alarm device off.

In this way, the logic circuit we designed uses Boolean algebra and logic gates to detect when a door or window is open and sound an alarm.

Review Questions

For Discreet Probability Distribution

1. A fair six-sided die is rolled once. Find the probability of rolling a 3.

2. A bag contains 5 red marbles and 3 blue marbles. If one marble is selected at random, find the probability that it is red.

3. A spinner is divided into 8 equal sections, numbered 1 through 8. If the spinner is spun once, find the probability of landing on an even number.

4. In a certain town, 70% of the residents own a car. If 5 residents are randomly selected, find the probability that at least 4 of them own a car.

5. A company produces light bulbs that have a lifetime that is normally distributed with a mean of 1000 hours and a standard deviation of 100 hours. Find the probability that a randomly selected bulb will last between 900 and 1100 hours.

6. A survey of 1000 adults found that 60% of them own a pet. If a group of 10 adults is randomly selected, find the probability that exactly 6 of them own a pet.

7. A card is drawn at random from a standard deck of 52 cards. Find the probability of drawing a heart or a diamond.

8. In a certain school, 20% of the students play a sport and 10% play a musical instrument. If 2 students are randomly selected, find the probability that both play a sport or both play a musical instrument.

9. A box contains 10 red balls and 5 blue balls. If 3 balls are drawn at random without replacement, find the probability that all 3 are red.

10. A fair coin is flipped 4 times. Find the probability of getting exactly 2 heads.

For Boolean Algebra and Logic Circuits

1. Simplify the Boolean expression: $(A + B)(A' + C)(B + C')$.

2. Simplify the Boolean expression: $A'B + AC' + AB'C$.

3. Create a truth table for the Boolean expression: $A'(B + C)$.

4. Simplify the Boolean expression: $(A + B')(B + C')(A' + C)$.

5. Draw the logic circuit for the Boolean expression: $A'(B + C)$.

6. Simplify the Boolean expression: $(A + B')(B + C)(A' + C') + AB'C$.

7. Create a truth table for the Boolean expression: (A + B')(B + C)(A' + C') + AB'C.

8. Simplify the Boolean expression: (A + B)(A' + C)(B + C') + A'B'C.

9. Draw the logic circuit for the Boolean expression: (A + B')(B + C)(A' + C') + AB'C.

10. Simplify the Boolean expression: A'B + A'C' + B'C.

CHAPTER FIVE

Topics in Discreet Mathematics

7. Matroid Theory

Matroid theory is a branch of discrete mathematics that studies mathematical structures called matroids. A matroid is a set with a certain property called the "matroid property," which is defined in terms of subsets of the set.

Formally, a matroid M is a pair (S, I), where S is a finite set and I is a collection of subsets of S called the "independent sets." The matroid property states that I satisfies the following axioms:

The empty set is an independent set.

Any subset of an independent set is also an independent set.

If A and B are independent sets with |A| < |B|, then there exists an element x in B - A such that (A U {x}) is also an independent set.

The third axiom is called the "exchange property" and is the defining characteristic of matroids. It states that if we have two independent sets A and B, where B is larger than A, we can always "exchange" an element from B for an element from A and still obtain an independent set.

Matroids have a wide range of applications in combinatorics, optimization, and algorithm design. They provide a powerful abstraction for many problems involving optimization, independence, and structure. Examples of matroids include graphic matroids, linear matroids, and binary matroids.

Matroid theory also studies properties of matroids, such as rank functions, bases, circuits, and duality. These concepts provide a rich framework for understanding the structure of matroids and developing algorithms for solving problems involving them.

Sample: Matroid Intersection

One important concept in matroid theory is the intersection of two matroids. Given two matroids $M1 = (S1, I1)$ and $M2 = (S2, I2)$, their intersection $M1 \cap M2$ is defined as the matroid $(S1 \cap S2, \{X \cap Y : X \in I1 \text{ and } Y \in I2\})$.

The matroid intersection has several useful properties, such as being a matroid itself and having a well-defined rank function. It also has applications in various areas of computer science, including algorithm design and optimization.

For example, suppose we have two sets of jobs J1 and J2 that need to be scheduled on a set of machines M. Each job j has a start time sj and a duration dj, and each machine m has a maximum capacity cm. We can model this problem as two matroids M1 = (J1, I1) and M2 = (J2, I2), where I1 and I2 are the collections of all sets of jobs that can be scheduled on machines with capacity at most c1 and c2, respectively.

To find a feasible schedule, we can take the intersection of M1 and M2 to obtain a new matroid M = (J1 ∩ J2, I), where I is the collection of all sets of jobs that can be scheduled on machines with combined capacity at most c1 + c2. This matroid corresponds to the set of all possible schedules that satisfy the capacity constraints.

We can then use standard matroid algorithms to find a maximum-weight independent set in M, where the weight of a set of jobs is the sum of their weights (e.g., the duration of the job). This gives us a feasible schedule with maximum total weight (i.e., the jobs with the highest priority).

In this way, the intersection of two matroids provides a powerful tool for solving optimization problems that involve multiple constraints and structures. Matroid theory offers a rich framework for developing algorithms that exploit these structures to achieve efficient and optimal solutions.

8. Game Theory

Game theory is a branch of mathematics that studies how individuals and groups make decisions in situations where their outcomes depend on the actions of others. It is used to model and analyze strategic interactions between rational decision-makers, such as players in a game, political parties in an election, or firms in a market.

In game theory, a game is a formal model of a situation where two or more players make decisions that affect each other's outcomes. Each player has a set of possible actions, and the game specifies how the outcomes depend on the actions of all players. The players are assumed to be rational and seek to maximize their own payoffs, which may depend on the actions of other players.

Game theory provides tools for analyzing and predicting the outcomes of such interactions, as well as for designing optimal strategies for the players. It also studies various concepts, such as Nash equilibrium, dominated strategies, and the prisoner's dilemma, which have important applications in economics, political science, and computer science.

One of the key insights of game theory is that rational players may not always achieve the best possible outcomes, especially when they are in a situation of mutual interdependence. For example, two competing firms may benefit more from cooperating and sharing the market than from engaging in a price war. However, the lack of trust and the fear of being exploited by the other party may lead them to choose a suboptimal strategy.

Game theory has many practical applications, including in economics, political science, psychology, biology, and computer science. It is used to study a wide range of phenomena, such as the evolution of cooperation, the design of auctions, the regulation of oligopolies, and the behavior of crowds and social networks.

An example of game theory is the Prisoner's Dilemma. In this scenario, two suspects are arrested and charged with a crime, but the police only have enough evidence to convict them on a lesser charge. The police offer each suspect a deal: if one suspect confesses and implicates the other, they will receive a reduced sentence, while the other suspect will receive a harsher sentence. If both suspects confess, they will each receive a moderate sentence, and if both remain silent, they will each receive a light sentence.

The game theory model assumes that the suspects are rational and seek to minimize their own sentence. The game is represented as a payoff matrix, where each cell represents the payoffs (sentences) for the two players based on their actions (confess or remain silent). In the Prisoner's Dilemma, the dominant strategy for each player is to confess, regardless of what the other player does.

This leads to a Nash equilibrium, where both players confess and receive moderate sentences, even though they would both be better off if they both remained silent and received light sentences. The game illustrates the concept of a collective action problem, where individual rationality leads to a suboptimal outcome for the group as a whole.

The Prisoner's Dilemma has many real-world applications, such as in international relations, where countries may face similar dilemmas in deciding whether to cooperate or compete with each other. Game theory provides a powerful framework for analyzing such situations and designing strategies that can lead to more optimal outcomes.

9. Optimization Techniques

Optimization techniques are a set of mathematical and computational methods used to find the best solution to a problem, given a set of constraints and objectives. Optimization problems are commonly found in many fields, including engineering, finance, logistics, and operations research.

There are various techniques for optimization, including linear programming, nonlinear programming, dynamic programming, stochastic programming, and metaheuristics. Each technique has its own strengths and limitations, and the choice of method depends on the nature of the problem and the available resources.

Linear programming is a common optimization technique used to optimize a linear objective function subject to linear constraints. It is often used in production planning, transportation optimization, and resource allocation problems.

Nonlinear programming is a more general optimization technique that can handle nonlinear objective functions and constraints. It is used in a wide range of applications, including portfolio optimization, chemical process design, and machine learning.

Dynamic programming is a technique used to solve optimization problems where the decision-making process involves multiple stages or steps. It is often used in operations research, economics, and engineering.

Stochastic programming is a technique used to optimize a decision-making process when there is uncertainty or risk involved. It is used in finance, insurance, and energy management.

Metaheuristics are a class of optimization techniques that use iterative search algorithms to find near-optimal solutions to complex problems. They are often used in optimization problems where the search space is very large or the problem is difficult to solve using other methods.

Optimization techniques are critical for solving complex problems in various fields. By finding the optimal solution, these techniques can help improve efficiency, reduce costs, and increase profitability.

One example of optimization techniques is the classic knapsack problem. In this problem, a knapsack with a maximum weight capacity is given, and there are a set of items with different weights and values. The goal is to select a subset of items that fit in the knapsack and maximize their total value.

This problem can be solved using integer programming, a branch of linear programming. The integer programming model can be formulated as follows:

Maximize:

$\sum_i v_i * x_i$

Subject to:

$\sum_i w_i * x_i <= W$, where $x_i \in \{0, 1\}$

where v_i is the value of the i-th item, w_i is the weight of the i-th item, W is the maximum weight capacity of the knapsack, and x_i is a binary decision variable indicating whether the i-th item is included in the knapsack ($x_i = 1$) or not ($x_i = 0$).

Solving this problem using integer programming can be computationally expensive for large problems, so metaheuristics such as genetic algorithms and simulated annealing can be used to find near-optimal solutions more efficiently.

Another example of optimization techniques is the traveling salesman problem. In this problem, a salesman must visit a set of cities and return to the starting city, while minimizing the total distance traveled. This problem can be formulated as an integer programming model or solved using metaheuristics such as ant colony optimization and tabu search. The solution to this problem has applications in logistics, transportation planning, and routing problems.

10. Computational Geometry

Computational geometry is a branch of computer science that deals with algorithms and data structures for solving geometric problems. These problems can involve points, lines, curves, surfaces, and higher-dimensional objects.

Computational geometry has numerous applications, including computer graphics, robotics, geographic information systems (GIS), and computer-aided design (CAD). Some of the key topics in computational geometry include geometric algorithms, convex hulls, triangulations, Voronoi diagrams, and Delaunay triangulations.

Geometric algorithms involve the computation of geometric properties such as distances, areas, and angles. These algorithms can be used to solve problems such as collision detection in robotics, proximity queries in GIS, and 3D modeling in computer graphics.

Convex hulls are a fundamental concept in computational geometry, and refer to the smallest convex polygon that contains a given set of points in the plane. Convex hull algorithms are widely used in GIS, computer vision, and pattern recognition.

Triangulations are another important concept in computational geometry, and involve dividing a geometric object into triangles. Triangulations have applications in computer graphics, mesh generation, and finite element analysis.

Voronoi diagrams are a type of partitioning of a plane into regions based on proximity to a set of points. Voronoi diagrams have applications in GIS, computer vision, and pattern recognition.

Delaunay triangulations are a special type of triangulation that satisfy a set of optimality conditions. They have applications in mesh generation, finite element analysis, and surface reconstruction.

Computational geometry is a rich and active research area, with numerous open problems and new applications emerging all the time.

One example of computational geometry is the problem of finding the intersection of two line segments in the plane. Given two line segments AB and CD, the goal is to determine whether they intersect, and if so, where.

One way to solve this problem is to use the cross product of vectors. Let AB and CD be represented as vectors a and b, respectively. Then the line segments intersect if and only if the cross product of a and b has a non-zero z-component, and the line segments are not parallel.

If the line segments intersect, we can compute the point of intersection by solving a system of linear equations. Let P be the point of intersection, and let s and t be the parameters such that $P = A + s(a - A) = C + t(b - C)$. Then we can solve for s and t using matrix algebra.

This problem has applications in computer graphics, collision detection, and robotics. For example, in a video game, we might want to determine whether a character has collided with an obstacle, and if so, at what point. By using computational geometry algorithms, we can efficiently solve this problem and make the game more realistic and engaging for the user.

Review Questions

For Matroid Theory

1. Let M be a matroid on a set E, and let A and B be two independent sets in M. Prove that there exists an element x in A such that A - {x} + B is still an independent set in M.

2. Let M be a matroid on a set E, and let r be the rank function of M. Prove that r is submodular, i.e., for any A and B in E, $r(A) + r(B) >= r(A \cup B) + r(A \cap B)$.

3. Let M be a matroid on a set E, and let C be a set of circuits in M. Prove that if C is minimally dependent, then each circuit in C is a basis of M.

4. Let M be a matroid on a set E, and let C be a set of circuits in M. Prove that if C is a basis of M, then each element in E belongs to exactly one circuit in C.

5. Let M be a matroid on a set E, and let A be a subset of E. Prove that A is independent in M if and only if for every subset B of A, we have $|B| <= r(B)$, where r is the rank function of M.

For Game Theory

1. Let M be a matroid on a set E, and let A and B be two independent sets in M. Prove that there exists an element x in A such that A - {x} + B is still an independent set in M.

2. Let M be a matroid on a set E, and let r be the rank function of M. Prove that r is submodular, i.e., for any A and B in E, r(A) + r(B) >= r(A ∪ B) + r(A ∩ B).

3. Let M be a matroid on a set E, and let C be a set of circuits in M. Prove that if C is minimally dependent, then each circuit in C is a basis of M.

4. Let M be a matroid on a set E, and let C be a set of circuits in M. Prove that if C is a basis of M, then each element in E belongs to exactly one circuit in C.

5. Let M be a matroid on a set E, and let A be a subset of E. Prove that A is independent in M if and only if for every subset B of A, we have |B| <= r(B), where r is the rank function of M.

For Optimization Technique

1. A company needs to ship 1000 units of product to three different cities. Each city has a different demand, and each truck has a different capacity. The cost of shipping each unit varies depending on the city and the truck used. Find the optimal shipping plan that minimizes the total cost.

2. A manufacturer needs to schedule production for five different products. Each product requires a different amount of time and resources to produce, and has a different profit margin. The manufacturer has a limited amount of time and resources available, and wants to maximize the total profit. Find the optimal production schedule.

3. A logistics company needs to plan the routes for its delivery trucks. Each truck can make multiple stops, and each stop has a different delivery time and cost. The company wants to minimize the total delivery time and cost. Find the optimal route plan.

4. A school needs to schedule classes for its students. Each student has a different set of required classes, and each class has a different teacher and room assignment. The school wants to minimize the number of conflicts between classes. Find the optimal class schedule.

5. A city needs to plan the locations of its emergency services, such as police stations, fire stations, and hospitals. Each service has a different response time and cost, and the city wants to minimize the total response time and cost. Find the optimal location plan.

For Computational Geometry

1. Given a set of n points in the plane, find the smallest convex polygon that encloses all the points. This problem is known as the convex hull problem and has applications in image processing, robotics, and computer graphics.

2. Given two line segments in the plane, determine whether they intersect or not. This problem is important in collision detection for computer graphics and robotics.

3. Given a set of n line segments in the plane, find all the intersections between the segments. This problem has applications in computer-aided design, geographic information systems, and computer graphics.

4. Given a set of n points in the plane, find the pair of points that are farthest apart. This problem is known as the maximum distance problem and has applications in clustering and pattern recognition.

5. Given a set of n points in the plane, find the smallest circle that encloses all the points. This problem is known as the minimum enclosing circle problem and has applications in robotics, computer graphics, and geographical information systems.

CHAPTER SIX

Topics in Discreet Mathematics

11. Algorithm Design and Analysis

Algorithm design and analysis is the process of designing and analyzing algorithms for solving computational problems. An algorithm is a step-by-step procedure for solving a problem, and algorithm design involves coming up with efficient and effective ways to solve problems using algorithms.

The analysis of algorithms involves studying the performance of algorithms in terms of their running time and space usage. This is important because different algorithms may have different running times and space requirements for the same problem, and it is often desirable to find algorithms that are both efficient and effective.

Some key techniques for algorithm design and analysis include dynamic programming, greedy algorithms, divide-and-conquer algorithms, and randomized algorithms. These techniques can be applied to a wide range of problems, from sorting and searching to optimization and graph theory.

Dynamic programming is a technique for solving problems by breaking them down into smaller subproblems and solving each subproblem only once. This can be used to solve problems such as finding the longest common subsequence of two strings or the shortest path in a graph.

Greedy algorithms are algorithms that make locally optimal choices at each step, with the hope of finding a global optimum. This technique is often used in optimization problems, such as the minimum spanning tree problem in graph theory.

Divide-and-conquer algorithms are algorithms that divide a problem into smaller subproblems, solve each subproblem independently, and then combine the solutions to the subproblems to obtain a solution to the original problem. This technique is often used in problems such as sorting and searching.

Randomized algorithms are algorithms that make use of randomization to improve their performance or find approximate solutions to problems. This technique is often used in problems such as graph coloring and clustering.

Algorithm design and analysis is a fundamental concept in computer science, and has applications in numerous fields, including data science, artificial intelligence, and computational biology.

One example of algorithm design and analysis is the problem of finding the shortest path between two nodes in a graph. This problem has applications in various fields such as transportation, network design, and communication networks.

One algorithm for solving this problem is Dijkstra's algorithm. The algorithm works by maintaining a set of visited nodes and an estimate of the shortest distance from the source node to each node in the graph. Initially, the estimate for the source node is zero, and the estimates for all other nodes are infinity. The algorithm then iteratively selects the node with the smallest estimate and updates the estimates for its neighbors. The process continues until the destination node is visited, or all reachable nodes have been visited.

The running time of Dijkstra's algorithm depends on the data structure used to maintain the estimates of shortest distances. If a binary heap is used, the algorithm has a running time of $O(|E| + |V| \log |V|)$, where $|V|$ is the number of nodes and $|E|$ is the number of edges in the graph.

Another algorithm for solving the shortest path problem is the Bellman-Ford algorithm. This algorithm works by relaxing edges repeatedly, relaxing an edge means updating the estimate of the shortest distance to a node if a shorter path is found. The algorithm repeats the relaxation process $|V| - 1$ times, where $|V|$ is the number of nodes in the graph. If after the $|V| - 1$ iterations, any further relaxation is possible, then there exists a negative weight cycle in the graph. The Bellman-Ford algorithm has a running time of $O(|V||E|)$.

Both algorithms have different strengths and weaknesses and are suitable for different scenarios depending on the properties of the graph. The choice of the algorithm is crucial for the performance of the application, and the analysis of the algorithm is essential for understanding its efficiency and correctness.

12. Machine Learning and Data Mining

Machine learning and data mining are two related fields that involve the use of algorithms and statistical models to discover patterns and make predictions based on data.

Data mining is the process of extracting useful information from large datasets. It involves techniques such as clustering, association analysis, and outlier detection, which can be used to identify patterns and relationships in data. Data mining can be applied to various fields such as finance, healthcare, and marketing, and is used to make data-driven decisions and improve business performance.

Machine learning is a subfield of artificial intelligence that focuses on developing algorithms that can learn from data and make predictions or decisions based on that data. Machine learning techniques include supervised learning, unsupervised learning, and reinforcement learning. In supervised learning, the algorithm is trained on a labeled dataset to make predictions on new, unseen data. In unsupervised learning, the algorithm is trained on an unlabeled dataset to find patterns and relationships in the data. Reinforcement learning involves training an agent to make decisions based on rewards or punishments received in a given environment.

Both data mining and machine learning rely on statistical techniques and algorithms such as regression analysis, decision trees, and neural networks. These techniques can be used to analyze large datasets, make predictions, and identify patterns that can be used to make data-driven decisions.

The applications of machine learning and data mining are numerous and include image and speech recognition, recommendation systems, fraud detection, and natural language processing. These fields are constantly evolving and advancing, with new algorithms and techniques being developed to improve their accuracy and effectiveness.

13. Network Flow Models

Network flow models are mathematical models used to describe the flow of resources through a network, such as water flowing through pipes, traffic flowing through highways, or data flowing through computer networks. The models can be used to optimize the flow of resources through the network by minimizing costs or maximizing efficiency.

The network flow model consists of a directed graph with nodes representing sources, sinks, and intermediate points in the network. The edges between nodes represent the flow of resources between them, and each edge has a capacity that represents the maximum flow that can pass through it.

There are several algorithms for solving network flow problems, such as the Ford-Fulkerson algorithm, the Edmonds-Karp algorithm, and the Dinic's algorithm. These algorithms work by iteratively finding augmenting paths, which are paths from the source node to the sink node that have available capacity. The flow along the augmenting path is increased until the capacity is reached, and the algorithm continues to find additional augmenting paths until no more paths can be found.

Network flow models have numerous applications in fields such as transportation, logistics, telecommunications, and computer networks. For example, in transportation networks, network flow models can be used to optimize the flow of goods or people through the network, while minimizing transportation costs. In computer networks, network flow models can be used to optimize the flow of data through the network, while minimizing network congestion.

Overall, network flow models are powerful tools for modeling and optimizing the flow of resources through a network, and they have many practical applications in various fields.

Let's consider an example of using network flow models in a transportation network. Suppose we have a network of roads that connect a set of factories to a set of warehouses. Each factory has a certain supply of goods, and each warehouse has a certain demand for those goods. Our goal is to transport the goods from the factories to the warehouses while minimizing the total transportation cost.

We can model this problem as a network flow model, where the factories are the source nodes, the warehouses are the sink nodes, and the roads between them are the edges. The capacity of each edge represents the maximum amount of goods that can be transported along that road, and the cost of each edge represents the cost of transporting one unit of goods along that road.

We can use the Ford-Fulkerson algorithm to solve this problem. The algorithm starts with an initial flow of zero and iteratively finds augmenting paths in the network until no more paths can be found. Each time an augmenting path is found, the flow along that path is increased by the minimum capacity of the edges along the path.

As the algorithm runs, the flow will increase until it reaches the maximum possible flow, at which point the algorithm terminates. The final flow represents the optimal transportation plan that minimizes the total transportation cost.

For example, suppose we have three factories (A, B, and C) and three warehouses (X, Y, and Z), and the transportation costs are as follows:

From A to X: cost 4, capacity 100

From A to Y: cost 5, capacity 80

From A to Z: cost 2, capacity 50

From B to X: cost 7, capacity 120

From B to Y: cost 6, capacity 90

From B to Z: cost 3, capacity 60

From C to X: cost 5, capacity 70

From C to Y: cost 4, capacity 100

From C to Z: cost 3, capacity 80

If we assume that each factory has a supply of 150 units and each warehouse has a demand of 100 units, we can solve the network flow model using the Ford-Fulkerson algorithm to obtain the optimal transportation plan that minimizes the total transportation cost.

14. Related Areas Of Computer Science And Engineering

Computer Science and Engineering is a vast field that includes several sub-disciplines and areas of research. Some of the related areas of Computer Science and Engineering are:

1. Artificial Intelligence: It is a subfield of Computer Science that focuses on creating intelligent machines that can simulate human behavior and thinking. AI techniques are used in various applications, including natural language processing, robotics, computer vision, and speech recognition.

2. Database Systems: It is a subfield of Computer Science that deals with the design, implementation, and management of large-scale data storage systems. It includes relational database management systems, NoSQL databases, and distributed database systems.

3. Computer Networks: It is a subfield of Computer Science that deals with the design, implementation, and management of computer networks. It includes topics such as network protocols, routing algorithms, wireless networks, and network security.

4. Operating Systems: It is a subfield of Computer Science that deals with the design, implementation, and management of computer operating systems. It

includes topics such as process scheduling, memory management, file systems, and device drivers.

5. Software Engineering: It is a subfield of Computer Science that deals with the design, development, and maintenance of software systems. It includes topics such as software design, software testing, software project management, and software quality assurance.

6. Computer Architecture: It is a subfield of Computer Science that deals with the design and construction of computer systems, including the design of processors, memory systems, and input/output devices.

7. Computer Graphics and Visualization: It is a subfield of Computer Science that deals with the creation, manipulation, and rendering of graphical images and animations. It includes topics such as 3D modeling, computer animation, and virtual reality.

8. Human-Computer Interaction: It is a subfield of Computer Science that deals with the design and

evaluation of user interfaces and interactive systems. It includes topics such as user interface design, usability testing, and user experience design.

As mentioned above are some subjects in university studies and in the academe which highlights the use of discreet mathematics.

In the next discussion we will focus on topics which are directly related to discreet mathematics and including some of their examples in relation to solving mathematical problems associated with discreet math.

Review Questions

For Algorithm Design and Analysis

1. Given a set of n integers, find the largest sum of any
   contiguous subarray. This problem can be solved using
   a dynamic programming approach with $O(n)$ time
   complexity.

2. Given a set of n points in the plane, find the pair of
   points that are closest together. This problem can be
   solved using a divide-and-conquer algorithm with $O(n
   \log n)$ time complexity.

3. Given a set of n elements and a target value, find the
   subset of elements that add up to the target value. This
   problem can be solved using a dynamic programming
   approach with $O(nW)$ time complexity, where W is the
   target value.

4. Given a set of n jobs with different processing times
   and deadlines, schedule the jobs to minimize the total
   number of late jobs. This problem can be solved using a
   greedy algorithm with $O(n \log n)$ time complexity.

5. Given a graph with n nodes and m edges, find the
   shortest path between two nodes. This problem can be
   solved using Dijkstra's algorithm with $O(m \log n)$ time
   complexity.

For Machine Learning

1. Given a dataset of n labeled examples, train a binary classifier to predict the label of a new example. This problem can be solved using logistic regression, which involves finding the optimal set of parameters that maximize the likelihood of the training data.

2. Given a dataset of n examples, cluster the examples into k groups based on their similarities. This problem can be solved using k-means clustering, which involves iteratively assigning examples to the nearest centroid and updating the centroids based on the mean of the assigned examples.

3. Given a dataset of n examples with missing values, impute the missing values to complete the dataset. This problem can be solved using matrix completion techniques, which involve estimating the missing values based on the observed values and the underlying structure of the dataset.

4. Given a dataset of n examples with multiple features, select the most informative features to use in a predictive model. This problem can be solved using feature selection techniques, which involve ranking the features based on their relevance and redundancy.

5. Given a dataset of n examples with non-linear relationships between the features and the labels, train a neural network to predict the labels of new examples. This problem can be solved using backpropagation, which involves computing the gradient of the loss function with respect to the weights of the network and updating the weights using stochastic gradient descent.

For Network Flow Models

1. Given a directed graph with edge capacities and two nodes s and t, find the maximum flow from s to t. This problem can be solved using the Ford-Fulkerson algorithm, which involves finding augmenting paths in the residual graph and updating the flow.

2. Given a bipartite graph with edge weights, find the maximum weight matching between the two partitions. This problem can be solved using the Hungarian algorithm, which involves finding an alternating path in the augmenting tree and updating the matching.

3. Given a directed graph with edge capacities and a set of node pairs with demands, find a feasible flow that satisfies the demands. This problem can be solved using the network simplex algorithm, which involves iteratively improving the flow by changing the node potentials.

4. Given a directed graph with edge capacities and a set of node pairs with costs, find a minimum-cost flow that satisfies the capacities. This problem can be solved using the cost-scaling algorithm, which involves iteratively scaling the capacities and finding the augmenting paths.

5. Given a directed graph with edge costs and a set of node pairs with capacities and costs, find a minimum-cost flow that satisfies the capacities and the costs. This problem can be solved using the primal-dual algorithm, which involves maintaining primal and dual solutions and iteratively updating them.

CHAPTER SEVEN

Topics in Discreet Mathematics

Discrete mathematics is a branch of mathematics that deals with mathematical structures that are discrete rather than continuous. Some of the important topics in discrete mathematics are:

1. Set Theory: It deals with the study of sets and their properties, including operations on sets, cardinality, and the axiom of choice.

2. Logic: It deals with the study of reasoning and argumentation. It includes propositional logic, predicate logic, and modal logic.

3. Graph Theory: It deals with the study of graphs and their properties, including graph connectivity, graph coloring, and graph algorithms.

4. Combinatorics: It deals with the study of counting and arrangements of objects, including permutation and combination, generating functions, and the principle of inclusion and exclusion.

5. Number Theory: It deals with the study of integers and their properties, including prime numbers, modular arithmetic, and number theoretic functions.

6. Probability Theory: It deals with the study of random events and their probabilities, including probability distributions, conditional probability, and stochastic processes.

7. Cryptography: It deals with the study of techniques for secure communication, including encryption algorithms, digital signatures, and cryptographic protocols.

8. Game Theory: It deals with the study of decision-making in strategic situations, including two-player games, Nash equilibrium, and social choice theory.

9. Information Theory: It deals with the study of communication systems and their capacity for transmitting information, including coding theory, source coding, and channel coding.

10. Algorithmic Graph Theory: It deals with the study of algorithms for solving problems on graphs, including matching algorithms, network flow algorithms, and graph coloring algorithms.

Below will be the sample computations on some of the discreet math problems with respect to the topics mentioned above.

1. Set Theory
   Example: Let A = {1, 2, 3} and B = {2, 3, 4}. Find A ∪ B and A ∩ B.

   Solution:

A ∪ B represents the union of sets A and B, which is the set of all elements that are in A or B or both.

A ∪ B = {1, 2, 3} ∪ {2, 3, 4} = {1, 2, 3, 4}

Therefore, the set A ∪ B contains all the elements that are in set A or set B or both.

A ∩ B represents the intersection of sets A and B, which is the set of all elements that are in both A and B.

A ∩ B = {1, 2, 3} ∩ {2, 3, 4} = {2, 3}

Therefore, the set A ∩ B contains all the elements that are in both set A and set B.

So, the final answers are:

A ∪ B = {1, 2, 3, 4}

A ∩ B = {2, 3}

2. Logic

Example: Determine the truth value of the following proposition: "If it rains, then the streets are wet."

Solution:

We can represent the proposition as a conditional statement with a hypothesis and a conclusion:

Hypothesis: It rains
Conclusion: The streets are wet

To determine the truth value of the proposition, we need to consider all possible cases:

If it rains and the streets are wet, then the proposition is true.

2.1 If it rains and the streets are not wet, then the proposition is false.

2.2 If it does not rain and the streets are wet, then the proposition is false.

2.3 If it does not rain and the streets are not wet, then the proposition is true.

Since the first case is the only one where the hypothesis is true and the conclusion is also true, the proposition is true.

Therefore, we can conclude that the proposition "If it rains, then the streets are wet" is true.

3. Graph Theory

Example: Consider the following graph:

A -- B -- C

| | |

D -- E – F

Find the shortest path from node A to node F using Dijkstra's algorithm.

Solution:

We can use Dijkstra's algorithm to find the shortest path from node A to node F. The algorithm works as follows:

3.1 Create a set of unvisited nodes and initialize the distance to A to 0 and the distance to all other nodes to infinity.

3.2 Select the node with the smallest distance as the current node (in this case, A).

3.3 For each neighbor of the current node, calculate the distance to that neighbor as the sum of the current node's distance and the weight of the edge between the two nodes.

3.4 If the calculated distance is less than the neighbor's current distance, update the neighbor's distance.

3.5 Mark the current node as visited and select the unvisited node with the smallest distance as the new current node.

3.6 Repeat steps 3-5 until the destination node (F) is visited or there are no more unvisited nodes.

Starting with node A, we can perform the following steps:

Distance to A: 0

Distance to B: infinity

Distance to C: infinity

Distance to D: infinity

Distance to E: infinity

Distance to F: infinity

The next node to visit is A with distance 0. From A, we can visit B and D with weights 1 and 1, respectively. Therefore, we update the distances:

Distance to A: 0 (visited)

Distance to B: 1

Distance to C: infinity

Distance to D: 1

Distance to E: infinity

Distance to F: infinity

The next node to visit is D with distance 1. From D, we can visit A and E with weights 1 and 1, respectively. However, the distance to A is already 0, so we don't need to update it. Therefore, we update the distances:

Distance to A: 0 (visited)

Distance to B: 1

Distance to C: infinity

Distance to D: 1 (visited)

Distance to E: 2

Distance to F: infinity

The next node to visit is B with distance 1. From B, we can visit A, C, and E with weights 1, 1, and 1, respectively. However, the distance to A and E is already 0 and 2, respectively, so we don't need to update them. Therefore, we update the distances:

Distance to A: 0 (visited)

Distance to B: 1 (visited)

Distance to C: 2

Distance to D: 1 (visited)

Distance to E: 2 (visited)

Distance to F: infinity

The next node to visit is C with distance 2. From C, we can visit B and F with weights 1 and 1, respectively. Therefore, we update the distances:

Distance to A: 0 (visited)

Distance to B: 1 (visited)

Distance to C: 2 (visited)

Distance to D: 1 (visited)

Distance to E: 2 (visited)

Distance to F: 3

The next node to visit is E with distance 2. From E, we can visit B and F with weights 1 and 1, respectively. However, the distance to B and F is already 1 and 3, respectively, so we don't need to update them. Therefore, we update the distances:

Distance

4. Combinatorics

Example: In how many ways can 5 people be seated in a row of 10 chairs if two of them refuse to sit next to each other?

Solution: Let's consider the two people who refuse to sit next to each other as a single entity. Then, we have 4 entities to arrange in a row of 10 chairs. The two people who refuse to sit next to each other can be arranged in 2 ways among themselves. Therefore, the number of ways to arrange the 5 people in a row of 10 chairs such that the two people who refuse to sit next to each other are not adjacent is:

4

!

×

2

=

48

$4! \times 2 = 48$

Therefore, there are 48 ways to arrange the 5 people in a row of 10 chairs such that the two people who refuse to sit next to each other are not adjacent.

5. Number Theory

Example: Determine whether 21 is a prime number or composite number.

Solution: A prime number is a positive integer greater than 1 that has no positive integer divisors other than 1 and itself. To determine whether 21 is a prime number or composite number, we need to check if it has any divisors other than 1 and itself.

We can start by checking the divisors of 21 up to the square root of 21, which is approximately 4.58. The divisors of 21 are 1, 3, 7, and 21. None of these divisors, except 1 and 21, are prime numbers. Therefore, 21 is a composite number since it has more than two positive divisors.

Alternatively, we can use the following theorem: A positive integer n is a prime number if and only if it is not divisible by any prime number less than or equal to the square root of n. Since the prime numbers less than or equal to the square root of 21 are 2 and 3, we can check if 21 is divisible by either of them. 21 is not divisible by 2 or 3, so it is a composite number.

Therefore, 21 is a composite number.

6. Probability Theory

Example: A bag contains 5 red balls, 3 blue balls, and 2 green balls. If a ball is drawn at random from the bag, what is the probability that it is blue?

Solution: The total number of balls in the bag is $5 + 3 + 2 = 10$. The probability of drawing a blue ball can be calculated as the number of ways to draw a blue ball divided by the total number of possible outcomes.

The number of ways to draw a blue ball is 3 (since there are 3 blue balls in the bag), and the total number of possible outcomes is 10 (since there are 10 balls in the bag). Therefore, the probability of drawing a blue ball is:

$$P(\text{blue}) = \tfrac{3}{10} = 0.3$$

Therefore, the probability of drawing a blue ball from the bag is 0.3 or 30%.

7. Cryptography

Sample 1: Caesar Cipher

The Caesar Cipher is one of the simplest and most widely known encryption techniques. It is a type of substitution cipher in which each letter in the plaintext is shifted a certain number of places down the alphabet.

Here's an example:

Plaintext: HELLO

Shift: 3

Ciphertext: KHOOR

In this example, each letter in the plaintext is shifted three places down the alphabet to get the corresponding letter in the ciphertext.

Solution:

To decrypt the ciphertext, you simply shift each letter in the opposite direction by the same number of places. So, to decrypt the ciphertext "KHOOR" with a shift of 3, you would shift each letter three places up the alphabet:

Ciphertext: KHOOR

Shift: 3

Plaintext: HELLO

Sample 2: RSA Encryption

RSA encryption is a widely used public-key encryption algorithm. It uses a pair of keys: a public key for encryption and a private key for decryption.

Here's an example:

Choose two distinct prime numbers p and q:

p = 11

q = 13

Calculate n = p * q:

n = 11 * 13 = 143

Calculate phi(n) = (p-1)(q-1):

phi(n) = (11-1)(13-1) = 120

Choose an integer e such that $1 < e <$ phi(n) and gcd(e, phi(n)) = 1:

e = 7

Compute the private key d such that (d * e) % phi(n) = 1:

d = 103

The public key is (n, e):

n = 143

e = 7

To encrypt a message m using the public key, compute c = m^e (mod n).

To decrypt the ciphertext c using the private key, compute m = c^d (mod n).

Solution:

Suppose we want to encrypt the message m = 9 using the public key (n, e) = (143, 7):

c = m^e (mod n)

c = 9^7 (mod 143)

c = 40

The ciphertext is 40.

To decrypt the ciphertext c = 40 using the private key d = 103:

m = c^d (mod n)

m = 40^103 (mod 143)

m = 9

The decrypted message is 9.

Note: This is a very basic example and in practice, RSA encryption uses much larger prime numbers to ensure the security of the encryption.

8. Game Theory

Here is an example of a game theory problem in discrete math, along with a solution:

Example:

Suppose there are two players, A and B, who each have two strategies to choose from: cooperate or defect. They are playing a game where the payoff matrix is as follows:

Player B

	Cooperate	Defect
Player A	+2, +2	-1, +3
	+3, -1	0, 0

In this game, the first number in each cell represents the payoff to player A, and the second number represents the payoff to player B. The values in each cell represent the payoffs in the order (cooperate, cooperate), (cooperate, defect), (defect, cooperate), and (defect, defect).

What are the Nash equilibria of this game?

Solution:

A Nash equilibrium is a set of strategies for which no player can increase their payoff by unilaterally changing their strategy. In other words, a Nash equilibrium is a stable state where neither player has an incentive to change their strategy.

To find the Nash equilibria of this game, we can look for any cells where neither player has an incentive to switch to the other strategy. These cells are marked with a plus sign (+) in the table.

The first cell in the table is a Nash equilibrium, since neither player has an incentive to switch to the other strategy. If player A chooses to cooperate, player B's best response is also to cooperate, since they both get a payoff of 2. Similarly, if player A chooses to defect, player B's best response is also to defect, since they both get a payoff of 0.

The second cell is also a Nash equilibrium, since again neither player has an incentive to switch. If player A chooses to cooperate, player B's best response is to defect, since they get a higher payoff of 3 instead of 2. But if player A chooses to defect, player B's best response is still to defect, since they get a payoff of 0 either way.

The third cell is not a Nash equilibrium, since player A has an incentive to defect if player B chooses to cooperate. If player B cooperates, player A's best response is to defect, since they get a higher payoff of 3 instead of 2. Similarly, if player B defects, player A's best response is to also defect, since they get a payoff of 0 either way.

The fourth cell is also not a Nash equilibrium, since player B has an incentive to defect if player A chooses to cooperate. If player A cooperates, player B's best response is to defect, since they get a higher payoff of 3 instead of 2. Similarly, if player A defects, player B's best response is to also defect, since they get a payoff of 0 either way.

Therefore, the Nash equilibria of this game are the first and second cells in the payoff matrix.

9. Information Theory

Here are two examples of problems in information theory along with their solutions:

Example 1: Binary Symmetric Channel

Suppose we have a binary symmetric channel with a crossover probability of $p = 0.1$. If we transmit a sequence of 10 bits, what is the probability that exactly 2 bits are received in error?

Solution:

Let X denote the number of bits received in error. Since this is a binary symmetric channel, we have:

$$P(X = k) = (10 \text{ choose } k) * p\char`^k * (1-p)\char`^(10-k)$$

For k = 2, we have:

P(X = 2) = (10 choose 2) * 0.1^2 * 0.9^8

= 45 * 0.01 * 0.43046721

= 0.193710645

Therefore, the probability that exactly 2 bits are received in error is approximately 0.1937.

Example 2: Entropy Calculation

Suppose we have a discrete random variable X with possible outcomes x1, x2, x3, x4, and probabilities P(X = xi) = pi for i = 1, 2, 3, 4. Calculate the entropy H(X) of this random variable.

Solution:

The entropy H(X) of a discrete random variable X with possible outcomes x1, x2, ..., xn and probabilities P(X = xi) = pi is defined as:

$H(X) = - \text{sum}(pi * \log2(pi), i = 1 \text{ to } n)$

Therefore, to calculate the entropy of X, we need to calculate pi * log2(pi) for each possible outcome xi, and then sum these values over all i. For the given random variable X, we have:

p1 = 0.3, p2 = 0.2, p3 = 0.25, p4 = 0.25

pi * log2(pi) for i = 1 to 4:

p1 * log2(p1) = 0.3 * -1.73696559 = -0.52108968

p2 * log2(p2) = 0.2 * -2.32192809 = -0.46438562

p3 * log2(p3) = 0.25 * -2 = -0.5

p4 * log2(p4) = 0.25 * -2 = -0.5

Therefore, the entropy of X is:

H(X) = -(-0.52108968 + (-0.46438562) + (-0.5) + (-0.5))

= 2.48687592

Therefore, the entropy of the random variable X is approximately 2.49 bits.

10. 10.   Algorithmic Graph Theory

Here is an example problem in algorithmic graph theory along with its solution:

Example: Minimum Spanning Tree

Consider the weighted graph G shown below:

```
    4   3
(1)--(2)--(3)
 | /\ |
5| / \ |6
 |/   \|
(4)--(5)--(6)
   2   7
```

Find the minimum spanning tree of G using Kruskal's algorithm.

Solution:

Kruskal's algorithm is a greedy algorithm that finds a minimum spanning tree of a connected, undirected graph G with weighted edges. Here are the steps to apply Kruskal's algorithm to the given graph G:

1. Sort the edges of G in non-decreasing order of their weights:

[(1, 2, 3), (4, 5, 2), (1, 4, 5), (2, 3, 3), (5, 6, 7), (2, 5, 6), (3, 6, 6)]

2. Initialize a set S of vertices with each vertex in its own subset.

3. Initialize an empty set T to be the minimum spanning tree of G.

4. For each edge (u, v, w) in the sorted list of edges:

   If u and v belong to different subsets in S, add (u, v, w) to T and merge the subsets of u and v in S.

   Otherwise, ignore (u, v, w).

5. Return T as the minimum spanning tree of G.

Applying Kruskal's algorithm to the given graph G, we obtain the following minimum spanning tree T:

```
    4    3

  (1)--(2)   (3)

        |\  |

       6| \ |5

        |  \|

  (4)--(5)--(6)

    2    7
```

The edges in T are:

[(4, 5, 2), (1, 2, 3), (2, 3, 3), (5, 6, 7), (1, 4, 5)]

Therefore, the minimum spanning tree of G is obtained by including the edges with weights 2, 3, 3, 5, and 5, which have a total weight of 18.

Other discreet math samples as follows.

Here are ten examples of problems in discrete math along with their solutions:

1. Combinatorics: How many ways are there to choose a committee of 3 people from a group of 10?

Solution: The number of ways to choose a committee of 3 people from a group of 10 is given by the combination formula: $C(10,3) = 10!/(3!7!) = 120$.

2. Probability: A coin is flipped 5 times. What is the probability of getting at least 3 heads?

Solution: The probability of getting at least 3 heads can be calculated as the sum of the probabilities of getting 3, 4, or 5 heads. The probability of getting exactly k heads in 5 flips is given by the binomial distribution: $P(k) = C(5,k) * (1/2)^5$. Therefore, the probability of getting at least 3 heads is $P(3) + P(4) + P(5) = C(5,3)(1/2)^5 + C(5,4)(1/2)^5 + C(5,5)*(1/2)^5 = 0.5$.

3. Set Theory: Let A = {1,2,3,4} and B = {3,4,5,6}. Find A ∩ B and A ∪ B.

Solution: A ∩ B is the set of elements that are common to both A and B, which is {3,4}. A ∪ B is the set of elements that are in either A or B, which is {1,2,3,4,5,6}.

4. Graph Theory: Consider the graph G shown below. Does G contain a Hamiltonian path?

1 -- 2 -- 3

  | | |

4 -- 5 – 6

Solution: A Hamiltonian path is a path that visits every vertex of a graph exactly once. In the given graph G, there is no Hamiltonian path because there is no path that visits all 6 vertices exactly once.

5. Logic: Write the negation of the statement "All cats are black."

Solution: The negation of the statement "All cats are black" is "There exists a cat that is not black."

6. Relations: Consider the relation R = {(1,2), (2,3), (3,4)} on the set {1,2,3,4}. Is R reflexive, symmetric, and/or transitive?

Solution: R is not reflexive because it does not contain the pairs (1,1), (2,2), (3,3), or (4,4). R is symmetric because if (a,b) is in R, then (b,a) is also in R. R is transitive because if (a,b) and (b,c) are in R, then (a,c) is also in R.

7. Functions: Let $f(x) = 3x + 1$ and $g(x) = x^2 - 2$. Find $(f \circ g)(x)$.

Solution: $(f \circ g)(x) = f(g(x)) = f(x^2 - 2) = 3(x^2 - 2) + 1 = 3x^2 - 5$.

8. Number Theory: Find the greatest common divisor (gcd) of 24 and 36.

Solution: We can use the Euclidean algorithm to find the gcd of 24 and 36: $gcd(24,36) = gcd(24,12) = gcd(12,0) = 12$.

Discrete mathematics has many practical applications in various fields, including computer science, cryptography, physics, engineering, and social sciences. Here are some of the main uses of discrete math:

Computer Science: Discrete math plays a central role in computer science, particularly in the design and analysis of algorithms, data structures, and computer networks. Concepts such as combinatorics, graph theory, set theory, and logic are essential in computer science.

Cryptography: Cryptography is the science of secure communication, and it heavily relies on discrete mathematics. Cryptography uses mathematical concepts such as number theory, modular arithmetic, and finite fields to encrypt and decrypt messages.

Physics and Engineering: Discrete mathematics is used extensively in physics and engineering to model physical systems, analyze data, and solve complex problems. Concepts such as graph theory, combinatorics, and probability theory are particularly useful in physics and engineering.

Social Sciences: Discrete math is also used in social sciences such as economics, sociology, and political science. Game theory, a branch of discrete mathematics, is used to model and analyze strategic interactions between individuals, firms, and governments.

Operations Research: Discrete math plays a significant role in operations research, which is the study of optimization and decision-making in complex systems. Operations research uses discrete mathematical concepts such as linear programming, network flows, and graph algorithms to optimize processes and systems.

In summary, discrete mathematics has a wide range of applications in various fields, and its importance continues to grow as technology and data analysis become increasingly important in our daily lives.

The future of discrete mathematics is promising, as the field continues to expand and find new applications in various areas. Here are some potential directions that the field may take in the future:

Applications in Artificial Intelligence: Discrete math concepts such as graph theory, probability theory, and game theory are critical in artificial intelligence and machine learning. As AI and machine learning become more prevalent, there will be increasing demand for experts in discrete mathematics.

Cryptography and Cybersecurity: With the increasing use of digital technologies and the internet, cybersecurity is becoming more critical than ever. Discrete math concepts such as number theory, modular arithmetic, and cryptography will continue to play a critical role in keeping our digital data and systems secure.

Data Science and Analytics: Discrete math concepts such as combinatorics and graph theory are essential in data science and analytics. As data becomes more abundant and complex, the need for experts in discrete mathematics to analyze and interpret the data will continue to grow.

Optimization and Decision-Making: Discrete math is fundamental to optimization and decision-making in various fields such as logistics, transportation, and finance. As these industries become more data-driven and complex, there will be an increasing need for experts in discrete mathematics to develop efficient algorithms and decision-making models.

In conclusion, the future of discrete mathematics is bright, as the field continues to find new applications and has a growing impact on various fields such as computer science, cryptography, data science, and optimization. As technology continues to evolve, the role of discrete math in our lives will only become more critical.

Review Questions

For Set Theory

1. The Continuum Hypothesis: This is a famous problem in set theory which asks whether there exists a set whose cardinality is strictly between that of the integers and that of the real numbers. This question was proved to be independent of the standard axioms of set theory (known as ZFC), which means that neither the Continuum Hypothesis nor its negation can be proved from the standard axioms.

2. The Axiom of Choice: This is a controversial axiom in set theory which states that given any collection of non-empty sets, there exists a way to choose one element from each set. While the Axiom of Choice is widely accepted and used in mathematics, it has also been the subject of much debate and controversy due to its counterintuitive consequences, such as the Banach-Tarski paradox.

3. Russell's Paradox: This paradox arises from the naive assumption that any definable property can be used to form a set. However, if we consider the set of all sets that do not contain themselves, we run into a contradiction: if this set contains itself, then it doesn't satisfy its defining property; but if it doesn't contain

itself, then it does satisfy its defining property. This paradox led to the development of more rigorous axioms for set theory.

4. The Large Cardinal Hypothesis: This is a family of conjectures which propose the existence of very large cardinals, which have properties that cannot be proved using the standard axioms of set theory. These conjectures have important consequences for the foundations of mathematics and for the study of infinity.

5. The Problem of Universals: This is a philosophical problem which arises in the context of set theory. It asks whether there exists a set of all possible properties or attributes, such as redness, roundness, or triangularity, that all objects can be said to possess. This problem has important implications for our understanding of the nature of reality and the relationship between language and the world.

For Logic Theory

1. The Decision Problem: This is the problem of determining whether there exists an algorithm that can decide, for any given logical statement, whether it is true or false. The problem was famously solved by Church and Turing, who proved that there is no

algorithm that can decide the truth of all statements in a certain type of logical system (known as first-order logic).

2. Gödel's Incompleteness Theorems: These theorems state that any formal logical system that is strong enough to express arithmetic must be either incomplete (i.e., there are statements that cannot be proved or disproved within the system) or inconsistent (i.e., it is possible to derive a contradiction within the system). These theorems have profound implications for the foundations of mathematics and the limits of formal reasoning.

3. Modal Logic: Modal logic is a branch of logic that deals with statements that express possibility, necessity, or contingency. It has many applications in philosophy, computer science, and artificial intelligence, but there are still many open problems in modal logic, such as the question of how to formalize notions like agency, time, and belief.

4. Non-Classical Logics: While classical logic is the dominant logical system in mathematics and philosophy, there are many alternative systems of logic that have been developed, such as intuitionistic logic, paraconsistent logic, and many-valued logic. These systems challenge some of the assumptions of classical

logic and have important implications for the foundations of mathematics and our understanding of reasoning.

5. Semantic Paradoxes: Semantic paradoxes are statements that seem to be self-contradictory when we consider their truth conditions. Examples include the liar paradox ("This statement is false") and the Russell paradox ("The set of all sets that do not contain themselves"). These paradoxes raise deep questions about the relationship between language, truth, and the world, and have led to the development of many non-classical logics and theories of truth.

For Graph Theory

1. The Four Color Theorem: This is a famous problem in graph theory which asks whether it is possible to color the regions of any map using only four colors, such that no two adjacent regions have the same color. The theorem was first stated in the 1850s and was finally proved in 1976 using a computer-assisted proof.

2. The Traveling Salesman Problem: This is a problem in graph theory which asks for the shortest possible route that a salesman can take to visit a given set of cities and return to his starting point. The problem is NP-hard,

which means that there is no known algorithm that can solve it efficiently for large numbers of cities.

3. Graph Coloring: Graph coloring is the problem of assigning colors to the vertices of a graph such that no two adjacent vertices have the same color. This problem has many practical applications, such as scheduling problems and register allocation in compilers.

4. Maximum Flow: Maximum flow is the problem of finding the maximum amount of material that can flow through a network of pipes or channels, subject to certain constraints. This problem has many practical applications, such as optimizing traffic flow and designing communication networks.

5. Ramsey Theory: Ramsey theory is the study of how order emerges from chaos in large, random systems. It has many applications in graph theory, combinatorics, and computer science. One of the most famous results in Ramsey theory is the Ramsey number, which gives the minimum number of nodes required in a complete graph to guarantee the existence of a subgraph of a certain size and structure.

For Combinatorics

1. The Riemann Hypothesis: This is one of the most famous unsolved problems in mathematics, and it has connections to combinatorics through the study of prime numbers. It states that all nontrivial zeros of the Riemann zeta function lie on the critical line with real part 1/2.

2. The Hadwiger-Nelson problem: This problem asks for the minimum number of colors needed to color the plane so that no two points at unit distance from each other are the same color. It is a famous open problem in combinatorial geometry.

3. The Lonely Runner Conjecture: This conjecture states that for any set of runners moving at different speeds around a circular track, there is always one runner who is "lonely" at some point during the race - that is, they are farther away from all the other runners than any other runner is at any given time.

4. The Strong Perfect Graph Conjecture: This conjecture states that every finite graph is either perfect or has an odd hole (an induced subgraph that is a cycle of odd length greater than or equal to 5) or an odd antihole (the complement of an odd hole). It is a major open problem in graph theory.

5. The Frankl Conjecture: This conjecture states that if a family of subsets of a finite set satisfies certain conditions, then it must contain a large subfamily that is either disjoint or has small pairwise intersections. It has connections to other areas of combinatorics, such as coding theory and designs.

Glossary

1. Set Theory: The branch of mathematics that deals with the study of sets, which are collections of objects.

2. Proposition: A statement that is either true or false.

3. Predicate: A proposition with variables that becomes a statement when specific values are assigned to the variables.

4. Proof: A logical argument that establishes the truth of a proposition.

5. Logical Connectives: Symbols or words used to combine propositions, such as "and" ($\wedge$), "or" ($\vee$), and "not" ($\neg$).

6. Truth Table: A table that shows all possible combinations of truth values for propositions and the resulting truth values of compound propositions.

7. Predicate Logic: A formal system that extends propositional logic to include quantifiers (such as "for all" ($\forall$) and "there exists" ($\exists$)).

8. Relations: A set of ordered pairs that defines a relationship between two sets.

9. Equivalence Relation: A relation that is reflexive, symmetric, and transitive.

10. Partial Order: A relation that is reflexive, antisymmetric, and transitive.

11. Graph Theory: The study of graphs, which consist of nodes (vertices) connected by edges.

12. Tree: A connected acyclic graph with no cycles.

13. Hamiltonian Path: A path in a graph that visits each vertex exactly once.

14. Eulerian Path: A path in a graph that visits each edge exactly once.

15. Combinatorics: The branch of mathematics concerned with counting and arranging objects.

16. Permutation: An arrangement of objects in a specific order.

17. Combination: A selection of objects without regard to order.

18. Pigeonhole Principle: A principle that states that if there are more pigeons than pigeonholes, then at least one pigeonhole must contain more than one pigeon.

19. Recursive Function: A function that is defined in terms of itself.

20. Cryptography: The study of secure communication and encryption methods.

These are just a few terms in discrete mathematics, and the field is vast with many more interesting concepts and terminologies to explore.

Reference

"This book is entirely sourced from ChatGPT, an artificial intelligence language model. All information and insights presented in this book have been generated by ChatGPT. The purpose of this book is to explore the capabilities of language models and their potential to generate informative and engaging content. All content in this book is cited appropriately to give credit to the source."

End of Book Disclaimer

The information and explanations provided in this book are based on the knowledge available up to September 2021. While efforts have been made to ensure the accuracy and reliability of the content, advancements and updates in the relevant fields may have occurred since the publication of this book. Therefore, readers are advised to consult the latest sources and references to obtain the most current and accurate information.

The author and publisher of this book disclaim any liability or responsibility for any loss or damage incurred by readers or users of this book, directly or indirectly, from the use of the information presented herein.

Warning from ChatGPT:

ChatGPT is an AI language model developed by OpenAI. It is designed to generate human-like text based on the input it receives. While ChatGPT strives to provide helpful and accurate information, it is important to note that it may not always generate correct or complete responses.

The responses generated by ChatGPT should not be considered as professional, legal, medical, or financial advice. Users should exercise caution and verify any information obtained from ChatGPT with reliable sources or consult with qualified professionals.

OpenAI, the creator of ChatGPT, cannot be held responsible for any actions, decisions, or consequences resulting from the use of ChatGPT.

Remember to use ChatGPT responsibly and critically evaluate the information it provides.

About the Authors

Cornelio Jeremy G. Ecle, is an avid research enthusiast and his research interest is in the area of alternative energy source, robotics engineering for medical applications, python and C++ programming, computer interface systems and many other technical research in engineering and allied sciences.

He is a graduate of Bachelor of Science in Electronics Communications Engineering from Cebu Institute of Technology University, Cebu City, Philippines.

He also holds a full pledge Masters in Information Technology from Asian Development Foundation College, Tacloban City, Philippines.

He is also a University Instructor at Eastern Samar State University, Salcedo Campus, Salcedo Eastern Samar, Philippines. He has been teaching in the university since 2012.

For your research related questions please email at jeremyecle2015@yahoo.com.

Arvin Anthony S. Araneta, is a researcher who conducts technical research in the areas of engineering and allied sciences.

He is graduate of Bachelor of Science in Computer Engineering from Eastern Samar State University, Main Campus, Borongan City, Philippines.

He also holds a full pledge Masters in Information Technology from Asian Development Foundation College, Tacloban City, Philippines.

He graduated as Doctor in Management Technology from Eastern Visayas State University. Tacloban City, Philippines.

He is also an Assistant Professor at Eastern Samar State University, Salcedo Campus, Salcedo Eastern Samar, Philippines.

Alma Padit Kuizon, is a researcher who conducts technical research in the areas of engineering and allied sciences.

She is a graduate of Bachelor of Science in Civil Engineering with License as a Registered Civil Engineer in the Philippines with other various Licenses and Registrations in the field of Geodetic and Civil Engineering.

She holds a full pledge Master's Degree in Mathematics.

She is also a graduate of Ph. D. in Mathematics.

She is also an Assistant Professor at Eastern Samar State University, Salcedo Campus, Salcedo Eastern Samar, Philippines.

Cherlowen A. Bolito, is a researcher who conducts technical research in the areas of engineering and allied sciences.

He is graduate of Bachelor of Science in Civil Engineering from Eastern Samar State University, Main Campus, Borongan City, Philippines.

He also holds a full pledge Masters of Arts Teaching Major in Mathematics from South Western University, Cebu City, Philippines.

He is also a University Instructor at Eastern Samar State University, Salcedo Campus, Salcedo Eastern Samar, Philippines.